How to ⓒ Write an Essay

Easy ways to write an essay especially for students using *English* as a first and second language.

Phil Rashid BA, Dip Eur Hum, CICT, TESOL

PARTRIDGE

A Penguin Random House Company

To order additional copies of this book, contact
Toll Free 800 101 2657 (Singapore)
Toll Free 1 800 81 7340 (Malaysia)
orders.singapore@partridgepublishing.com

www.partridgepublishing.com/singapore

Forward

Learning English as a second language, or even a third language, can be daunting for you, as students. I want to allay the fears that confront you. This book will show you that, by applying the recommended methods, from the initial first written title to the final concluding paragraph, you will eventually find a clear way of essay construction.

I hope you will enjoy future essay writing after mastering the techniques learnt from the instructions, portrayed in this book.

HAPPY WRITING

Phil Rashid

I dedicate this book to

my son **Daniel**

my daughter **Aishah**

and

my grandson **Aiden**

I thank them all
for giving me
the inspiration
needed to write it.

May they and others
benefit from
the knowledge
it may
give them.

I would also like to thank
**Sekolah Kebangsaan
Puncak Alam 3,**
Selangor Darul Ehsan,
Malaysia,
for allowing me to photograph
a classroom with their students.

SYMBOL	ERROR	CORRECTION
1. **SVA** SINGULAR - PLURAL	He **hath** been here for six **month.**	He **has** been here for six **months.**
2. **WF** WORD FORM	I saw a **beauty** picture.	I saw a **beautiful** picture.
3. **WC** WORD CHOICE	She got **on** the taxi.	She got **into** the taxi.
4. **VT** VERB TENSE	He **is** since June.	He **has been** since June.
5. **^** ADD A WORD	I want ^ go to the zoo.	I want **to** go to the zoo.
6. _ OMIT A WORD	She entered <u>to</u> the university.	She entered the university.
7. **WO** WORD ORDER	I saw **five times that movie.**	I saw **that movie five times.**
8. **INC.** INCOMPLETE	**Because I was tired.**	**I went to bed**, because I was tired.
9. **SP** SPELLING	An accident **hapened.**	An accident **happened.**
10. **P** PUNCTUATION	What did he say	What did he say**?**
11. **C** CAPITALISATION	I am an **e**nglishman.	I am an **E**nglishman.
12. **@** ARTICLE	I had **a** accident.	I had **an** accident.
13. **?** UNCLEAR MEANING	He borrowed a **writing thing.**	He borrowed a **pen.**
14. **RP** REPHRASE	Playing football **can exercise body.**	Playing football **is a good way to exercise the body.**

Contents

Chapter One

CAPITALISATION

Capital **L***etters*

Articles

Prepositions

and

Conjunctions

CAPITALISATION Rules

Rule 1. **Capitalise** the first word of a quoted sentence.
Example: He said, *"Treat her as you would your own daughter"*.

Rule 2. **Capitalise** a person's title, when it precedes the name. Don't capitalise when the title is acting as a description following the name. Example: *Chairperson Petrov. Ms.Petrov, the chairperson of the is here.*

Rule 3. **Capitalise** a proper noun. Example: *Tower Bridge.*

Rule 4. **Capitalise** when the person's title follows the name on the address or signature line. Examples: *Sincerely Ms. Haines, Chairperson*

Rule 5. **Capitalise** the titles of high-ranking government officials when used with or before their names. Do not capitalise the civil title if it is used instead of the name. Example:
The prime minister will address Parliament.
All members of Parliament are expected to attend.

Rule 6. **Capitalise** any title used as a first address. Example: *"Will you take my temperature, Doctor?"*

Rule 7. **Capitalise** points of a compass, only when they refer to specific regions.
Example: *We live in the southeast region of the town. Because southeast* is just an adjective, describing a section it **should not** be capitalised.

Rule 8. **Capitalise** Always capitalise the first and last words of publication titles regardless of their parts of speech. Always capitalise other words within titles, including the short verb forms **Is**, **Are** and **Be**. Don't capitalise **words within titles** such as, a, an, the , but, as, if, and, or, nor, or any prepositions, regardless of their length.
Examples: *The Day of the Jackal, A Tale of Two Cities*

Rule 9. **Capitalise** *federal* or *state* when used as part of an official agency name or in documents wh these terms represent government an official name. If they are being used as general terms lower-case letters may be used. Examples: *The state has evidence to the. contrary, that it's a federal offence. The State Board collects sales taxes.*

Rule 10. **Capitalise** words such as department, bureau and office if you have prepared your text in the following way.
Example: The **B**ureau of **L**and **M**anagement (**B**ureau) has some jurisdiction over **I**ndian lands.

Rule 11 **Capitalise** names of seasons, is wrong.
Example: *I love autumn colours. The first day of spring is almost here.*

Rule 12. **Capitalise** the first word of a salutation and the first word of a complimentary close.
Examples: **D**ear **M**s Mohammed: **M**y dear **M**r Sanchez: **V**ery truly yours.

Rule 13. **Capitalise** words derived from proper nouns. Examples *I must take English and maths. English* is capitalised, because it comes from the proper noun, *England,* but *maths* does not come from *mathland.*

Rule 14. **Capitalise** the names of a specific course titles. Example: *I must take History and Geography.*

CAPITAL *LETTERS / Articles*

We use *capital letters* . . . .

with names   Jackie Chan; Michael Jackson
at the beginning of a sentence Hello. **My** name's **Paul**. **W**hat's your name?
with I   **I**'m James.

Write *a / an / the* in the correct place.

1. Could I have _____ drink of water please?
2. I'm staying in _____ small hotel. _____ one over there.

Re-write the sentences with *capital letters*.

a. his name's tony. he's an actor. _____ .
b. my name's phil. i'm a teacher. _____ .

CAPITAL *LETTERS / Prepositions*

Aa Bb Cc Dd **Ee** F Gg Hh **Ii** Jj Kk Ll Mn Nn **Oo** Pp Qq Rr Ss Tt **Uu** Vv Ww Xx Yy Zz

We use *capital letters* . . . .

with towns and cities   London; **B**eijing; **T**okyo; **K**uala **L**umpur.
with countries   **S**audi **A**rabia; **S**outh **K**orea; **Y**emen.
with nationalities   **L**ibyan; **D**jiboutian; **M**ongolian.
Write the *preposition*:

         + school; university
 at   Ahmed is studying **at** a language school.
         China
 from   She's **from** China.
         + city/country
 in   London is **in** England.
 on   They're **on** holiday.

Write the correct ***preposition*** in the space.

1. I'll have lunch _____ work. 3. He's the spy. He's _____ surveillance.
2. Where's Tokyo. It's _____ Japan. 4. You will find it_____ the bank.

Re-write the sentences with *capital letters*.

1. thiery henri is a french footballer. _____ .
2. beijing is the capital of china. _____ .

CONJUNCTIONS

Conjunction words are used to *connect sentences*. They *can agree* with a sentence or *change the meaning*.
Write the correct conjunction word: **and / but** on the lines between the sentences. They take the place of
periods and capital letters. Re-write the sentences underneath.

We are going on holiday. _____ My dad is staying here at home.

_____

My mum can drive a car. _____ My mum is a good cook.

_____

A, An, The

_____   _____   _____   _____

Write the following names under the above pictures:-

1. an exercise bike   2. a chair   3. a rabbit   4. an elephant

An is used because of the way a word sounds. **These are called VOWELS**

hour

honour

} both have their first letter (h), a consonant, which is silent.

A – is used as a pre-fix before nouns that begin with all the other letters.
These are called CONSONANTS
We use it for singular or countable nouns that don't begin with the above letters.
They are also used because of the way they sound. (The sound of these vowels)

universe

unity

} both have their first letter, (u) a vowel, sounding like a *consonant* **NOT** a *vowel*.
U sounds like you.

Therefore, when speaking   –   "It is **an h**onor to meet you."

"See you in **an h**our."

"We are studying in **a u**niversity."

These words, **a / an,** are called *indefinite articles.*

When we speak about all *nouns, vowels and consonants,* for a second time, we promote them.

to **THE**

The man.   **The** woman.   **The** orange.   **The** anniversary

Or, if there is only one of a kind.

The Pacific Ocean   **The** sky   **The** moon   **The** earth

These are called *definite articles,* because they are very specific.

Complete the sentences with *PREPOSITIONS* that describe the pictures.

Write each *preposition* – once (using the **capital letter***)*, in the boxes.

A bear is ☐ *Aishah*'s lap. A bear is ☐ *Aishah*'s legs. *Aishah* is ☐ a bear, *Aishah* is ☐ a bear, *Aishah* is ☐ a bear, *Aishah* is ☐ two bears.

A- next to; **B**-in; **C**-in front of; **D**-on; **E**-above; **F**-between

Prepositions

1. My best friend lives _____ Malaysia.
   a. on
   b. in
   c. at

2. Since he met his new friend, he   doesn't seem to be _____ home.
   a. at
   b. with
   c. on

3. I'll be ready to leave ,_____ a few minutes.
   a. on
   b. in
   c. since

4. The child responded to her mother's demands, _____ a tantrum.
   a. on
   b. about
   c. with

5. I think she spends all her time _____ the phone.
   a. on
   b. in
   c. at

6. I will wait_____ 9.30 but then I'm going home.
   a. in
   b. until
   c. at

7. The constable caught the thief _____ the corner, of the post office.
   a. about
   b. in
   c. at

8. I couldn't come so my dad, wrote a note_____ me.
   a. by
   b. for
   c. at

9. I'm not interested, _____ buying a new car now.
   a. in
   b. for
   c. on

10. What are the ingredients _____ this cake?
    a. about
    b. to
    c. in

11. My daughter is named_____ an important Muslim lady.
    a. with
    b. for
    c. after

12. I watched TV   ____ two in the morning.
    a. in
    b. for
    c. until

13. Students learn English _____ enroll into a university.
    a to
    b in
    c by

14. You can buy things _____ credit card.
    a on
    b at
    c with

Punctuation

When people speak to each other, they usually make gestures with their hands to determine the emphasis *pauses* needed on certain words and phrases. When we write words down, we also need to indicate when these *pauses* should occur, otherwise our writing would simply be, a long stream of words. In the English language I have chosen six pieces of punctuation to help you. Two are *punctuation marks* that indicate a *pause*: these are **full-stops and commas.** The other four are the **inverted commas, apostrophes, brackets** and **hyphens.**

The Full Stop (.)

You must **always** end a sentence with a full stop. This rule must **always** be obeyed. After the *full stop* the next sentence **must start** with a capital letter. *Full stops* can be used after an abbreviation. However, when a full stop follows an abbreviation you **do not** use a capital letter, unless you are starting a new sentence or unless the next word naturally begins with a capital letter. For instance:

The months of the year, January, February, March etc.
may be abbreviated to Jan; Feb; Mar.

Notice that after etc. there is no capital letter, but the months start with capital letters because their full forms have capitals. Also notice that at the end of the sentence there is only one *full stop*. Never use two *full stops*.

The Comma (,)

The *comma* is punctuation mark which indicates the shortest pause. It is best to write short sentences with a more direct approach to a subject.
Commas also mark off the items in a list:
There were a lot of strawberries, apples, pears, bananas and cherries on the table.

Inverted Commas (" ")

They are used to indicate direct speech. Use the single for quotations.
   i)   *The students said, "We really like your book."*
  ii) A quote from the book, *'I hope that this book has enlightened you.'*

The Apostrophe (')

The apostrophe is used when a letter is missed from a word:-
   i)   *It's not the one. It is not the one.*   ii)   *It doesn't fit. It does not fit.*
You also use it to show ownership. Simply add the letter **s:**
   i)   *The girl's room.*   ii)   *The girls' room.*
  Singular.   (belonging to the girl)   Plural.   (belonging to the girls)

Brackets ( )

Brackets are usually wrapped around a phrase or statement inserted into a sentence.
The cost of the book will be $16.00 (inclusive of postage and packing).

The Hyphen (-)

Don't confuse a hyphen with a dash. A dash lengthens a pause, between words, a hyphen shortens it.
    son-in-law   *court-martial*   *men-at-arms*   *three-o-clock*
They are also used to alter the meaning of words.
   i)   *He recovered his lost and torn umbrella.*
  ii)   *His torn umbrella was then* **re-covered***.*

I Want to Be a Good Student

Change lower case letters to upper case letters and punctuate wherever necessary in the following essay.

capital letter

capital letter   *full stop*   *apostrophe*   *comma*

Make sure you pay attention in class. You mustn't start talking on your mobile, to your friends, especially when your teachers have their backs turned to you.

comma   *full stop*

you also must not be involved with distracting people you should understand that the people in your class play an important role in how you and everybody else progresses however if you are a good student you can do better and achieve your goals your friends will be much more appreciative of you if you show a good example at home study and do your homework in a place that doesnt make you sleep stay away from the tv radio stereos however some students find soothing music a benefit it is also advisable to have a study table or desk in a room designated for studying this would be a very good idea because it will help you concentrate on your studies

if you feel distracted take a short break of 15 minutes or less maybe try to read an unrelated story book but dont get hooked to the book if the time limit is over book mark the page and then you can read it later on you should also have a daily routine timetable to guide you but you must follow it through

dont cheat by copying from your colleague .always remember cheating will make you lose your friends answer may not always be the right answer it could be wrong its best therefore to go with your first instinctive idea you will probably find that if you have faith in your own abilities it will usually be the correct answer dont cheat be honest if you dont know the answer leave it dont dwell on a question move on if you are not sure make sure you try to answer all the questions in an exam exams are set up for students to also test their time management as well as their knowledge return to questions you are unsure of when you have initially finished an exam remember study well now and you can have fun after you achieve your goal guaranteed good luck

Chapter Two

Introductory Paragraphs

The Introductory Paragraph

The first paragraph in an essay is very important. It is composed of sentences that will lead the reader into the rest of the essay. A good introduction will entice the reader to read on, a window that will further open the mind. Therefore, the introduction has a double purpose, to introduce the essay topic to the readers and to get their attention.

The paragraph has to be very general, not specific. To this end, use words and phrases that are non-specific. Do not use *pronouns* such as my; our; their; your; his and her. *Determiners* such as many; some; quite a few and not many, should be used. These are general and non-specific and will not give a direct viewpoint to any chosen topic.

Question words are very helpful in creating an *introductory paragraph*. They can also be used to construct sentences in all *paragraphs*.

Question - words	Usage	Example
1. *Where* (area)	Asks about the place of an event or action.	**Quite a lot** of events happen in my city. **Some** can occur at the same place.
2. *Who* (person/s)	Asks about people.	**Many** people live in different habitats. **Some** people could not live in the same environment.
3. *Which* (selection)	Asks about people places and kinds.	**Some** people have indigenous tastes. **Not many** may want to live near a coast.
4. *What* (subject)	Asks about people animals and habitats.	**Many** floods have destroyed many animals' habitats. **Some** people live in strange habitats.
5. *When* (time)	Asks about the time of events.	**Quite a few** anniversaries are a time of celebration. **Many** schedules must always be kept.
6. *Why* (reasons)	Asks for reasons why things happen.	**A lot of** unreliable transport causes **some** people to be late. **Many fathers** are late, caused by traffic jams.
7. *How* (method)	Asks about the manner in which an action is performed.	**A lot of people** relax by playing sports. **Some** families employ maids to help with housework.

Exercise
Circle the best answer. Then **write the answer** in the **blank spaces.**

1. _____ is the book?
   a. When   c. Why
   b. Where   d. How
   Not as good as the film.

2. _____ is your father's occupation?
   a. When   c. Why
   b. What   d. Who

3. _____
   is the toy? It is the bag.
   a. When   c. Why
   b. Where   d. How

4. _____
   is your mother?
   a. When   c. Why
   b. What   d. How

5. _____
   did you get here?
   a. Who   c. What
   b. Where   d. How

6. _____are you studying?
   The English language.
   a. When   c. Why
   b. What   d. How

7. _____will you come home? Tonight.
   a. When   c. Why
   b. Where   d. What

8. _____ are you feeling?
   a. When   c. Why
   b. Where   d. How

9. _____ are you phoning? My dad.
   a. Who   c. Why
   b. Where   d. How

10. _____is the bank?
    That one.
    a. When   c. Why
    b. Which   d. How

11. _____are you doing?
    a. When   c. Why
    b. Where   d. What

12. _____is it closing?
    At 3.00 pm.
    a. When   c. Where
    b. Why   d. How

13. _____are you coming?
    a. When   c. Where
    b. Why   d. How

14. _____ is that man?
    That's my brother.
    a. When   c. Who
    b. Why   d. How

Quantifiers: a few - many - a lot of   *a little - much - not much*

Countable	Uncountable
A lot of glasses.	*Much* money.
A few cookies.	*A little amount* of honey.
Many containers	*Not much* milk.
A few mugs.	*A little amount of* salt.

Complete the sentences with:
a few / many / a little amount of / much / not much / a lot of

1. My grandmother has made so _____ jars of jam for all of us.
2. There isn't _____milk in the fridge.
3. They only drank _____ cans on holiday.
4. There are _____ bears now in the park.
5. There's_____ money left after spending so _____at the shops.
6. Are there _____more balloons to be blown up?
7. Please buy _____jam to put on the toast.
8. We only ate _____cookies before tea.
9. All you need is_____ to add to the soup.
10. _____ of us are going out tonight.

Introduction Paragraph Construction

Signal Words/Phrases

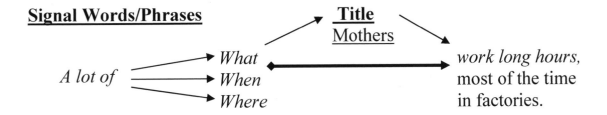

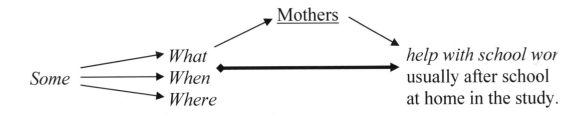

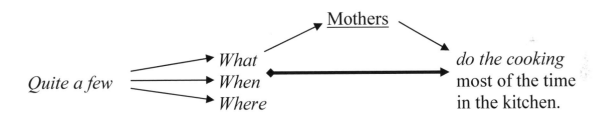

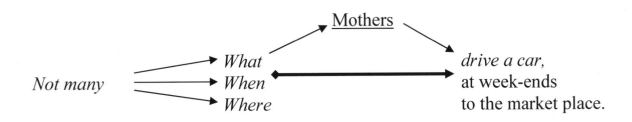

Titles and Introductions

My Family — **Parents**

My Family — **Siblings**

The *fathers* and *mothers* are the backbone to any family. *The siblings,* if any, also help to bond the family unit together. The *father usually* makes the decisions. *Mothers* will *always* maintain an orderly house. The *father rarely* cleans the house but *sometimes* might cook. The *siblings,* when able, will also help share in house duties.

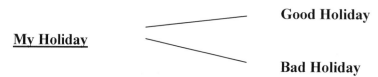

My City and Kuala Lumpur — **London**

My City and Kuala Lumpur — **Beijing**

Many cities have similar buildings. *Some* people of similar cities speak the same language. *A lot of* cities have rivers flowing through them. *Quite a few* cities have famous statues and buildings in them.

My Holiday — **Good Holiday**

My Holiday — **Bad Holiday**

Many people go, or would like to go on a holiday. There are *many* reasons for doing so. They may be personal or just for the experience. When they return, *most* people will have unforgettable experiences. *Some* people will have good times to remember. However, others will not be so fortunate.

A Chosen Celebrity — **Singers**

A Chosen Celebrity — **Actors / Actresses**

Celebrities are such because they are famous. *Many* would not be called such if a few people knew them. *However* even though they could be world-known, they might be non-entities to *some* people. They are *usually* recognized when they come on TV. This is because of the exposure they will receive. Actors, actresses and sportsmen will *always* be recognized as well as singers and pop-stars.

Introduction Paragraph Construction

Write the *titles* that you choose and construct the *Introduction Paragraphs,* using the signal phrases, below. Refer to the samples on **pages 13 and 14.**

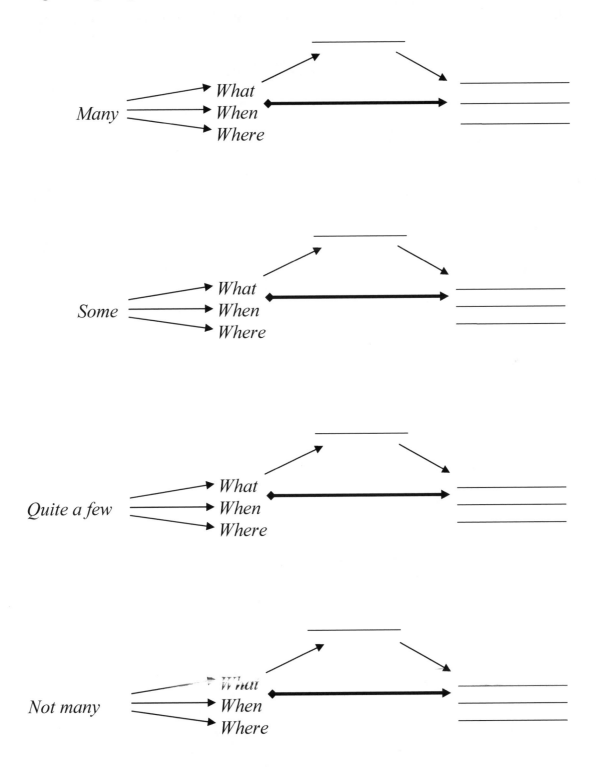

Frequency Adverbs Table

	Mon	Tue	Wed	Thu	Fri	Sat	Sun
Amir **ALWAYS** eats pizza.	🍕	🍕	🍕	🍕	🍕	🍕	🍕
Justin **USUALLY** eats pizza.		🍕	🍕	🍕	🍕	🍕	🍕
Jane **OFTEN** eats pizza.			🍕	🍕	🍕	🍕	🍕
Bob **SOMETIMES** eats pizza.				🍕	🍕	🍕	🍕
Phil **SELDOM** eats pizza.						🍕	🍕
Daniel **RARELY** eats pizza.							🍕
Abdul **NEVER** eats pizza.							

This is very useful in determining how your sentences will progress. Use them to emphasise what is happening at certain times: My father **always** has breakfast. My mother **never** drives the car.

Titles and _Introductions_
My Parents

_____

_____

_____

_____

How to Improve My School

_____

_____

_____

_____

Chapter Three

The

Thesis

Statements

Rules for *Thesis Statements* (propositions or dissertations)

1. A *thesis statement* must be a statement, **NOT a question.**

2. A *thesis statement* must be a complete sentence. This means that it must have a **subject** and a **verb.**

3. A *thesis statement* **cannot be a simple statement of *fact.*** A *fact* doesn't need any support, therefore you cannot write an essay about it.

4. A *thesis statement* must **state the controlling idea,** not just wonder whether or not if something is true. This means that you must state your position on the *topic*; you simply cannot make an announcement of what you are going to write in the essay.

5. A *thesis statement* should **trigger an argument;** it should leave space for people to be for or against it. It should not present a stance that everybody agrees upon.

- Which of the sentences below are *thesis statements?*
- Put a check mark (✓) next to those you think are *thesis statements.*
- If you think the sentence is not a *thesis sentence,* write the number of the rule it violates, in the box, next to it.

A	Japanese cars are better than American cars.	
B	A Proton is a Malaysian car.	
C	I am going to show you that seat belts are necessary.	
D	Are seat belts necessary?	
E	Seat belts save lives and money.	

Thesis Statement Construction

Sometimes, a subject has to go through several stages of limiting, before it is narrow enough to write. Below are four lists that were written through before being narrowed down to a *thesis statement*. Put each list in order of rank. This is to help identify the priority in writing the subjects from the main point. This will also culminate into the broader points of the *title.* The stages can be used as simple plans to help construct introductory sentences.

List One

_____Teachers.

1
_____Education.

_____Professors.

_____Good and bad
Teachers.

_____High school
Teachers.

List Two

_____Bicycles.

_____Dangers of
bike riding.

_____Recreation.

2
_____Recreational
vehicles.

_____Advantages and
disadvantages
of bike riding.

List Three

_____Advantages and
disadvantages of.
working in a bank.
_____Banks.

_____Dealing with customers.

3
_____Working in a bank.

_____Financial institutions.

List Four

_____Camping.

4
_____First camping trip.

_____Summer vacations.

_____Vacations.

_____Advantages and
disadvantages
of camping.

The *Thesis Statement*

There are many ideas on how a good *thesis statement* should be composed. Writers should decide on whether they want to construct a weak or strong one. For the benefit of new students, I am only going to concentrate on *thesis statements* that you will not only understand, but will enable you to construct them easily for yourselves. When you get to a higher level you may want to elaborate further.

The important thing to remember is that your *thesis statement* needs to show ideas about a subject. The composition, like the paragraphs, is controlled by one central idea: The *Thesis Statement.* It is a one-sentence summary of the whole composition.

Here are some examples of *thesis statements*:-

1. This essay will discuss the *advantages and disadvantages* of having parents and siblings
2. In this essay I will discuss the *advantages and disadvantages* of having lived in two countries.
3. There are both *advantages and disadvantages* of living away from home.
4. There are advantages and disadvantages to owning your own car
5. In this essay I will discuss the *advantages and disadvantages* of being married.
6. In this essay I will discuss the *advantages and disadvantages* of having to go without water.

Thesis statements can also allow the writer to write two sub-*topic sentences* that can have paragraphs relating to the main *topic.*

For example:-

<u>My Family</u>

1. **My family** *are always supported by my parents.*

   My father is *a hardworking man.*

   My mother, *at home* is *a very good cook.*

2. **My family** *always has sports-minded children.*

   My brother and I, every week-end, play *football*

   My sisters *are* in the *volleyball and netball teams.*

The Difference Between a *Thesis Statement* and a *Topic Sentence.*

The **thesis statement** governs the whole content of the whole composition.
The **topic sentence** only governs the development of *one paragraph.*
The **thesis statement** also points to a landmark or landmarks along the way.

Thesis statements, point to the ultimate destination, of an essay.

Example 1 :-SUBJECT	VERB	TOPIC
In this essay I	will discuss	the ***advantages and disadvantages*** *of owning a car.*

Example 2 :-SUBJECT	VERB	TOPIC
In this essay I	will discuss	the ***advantages and disadvantages*** of being married.

Example 3 :-SUBJECT	VERB	TOPIC
Living away from home.	has	***advantages and disadvantages.***

Topic **sentences**, should introduce the main idea of the paragraph.

	SUBJECT	VERB	OPINION	TOPIC
Body	i) Owning a house	has	many	***advantages.***
Paragraph 1	ii) Owning a car	has	several	***advantages.***

Look, forward, to pages **43-44,** to see how *transition signals* can be used to emphasize the differences between the *topics.*

Body Paragraph 2	i) However, has owning a house	also many	***disadvantages.***
	ii) However, has owning a car	also several	*disadvantages.*

More Examples 0f Differences Between
Thesis Statements and *Topic Sentences.*

Write *your own* **thesis** examples in the spaces provided and two supporting topics.

	SUBJECT	VERB	THESIS
Example :-	This essay	will discuss	the **advantages** *and* **disadvantages** of being married.

	SUBJECT	VERB	THESIS STATEMENT

a) _____ .

	SUBJECT	VERB	TOPICS

b) _____ .

c) _____ .

Topic sentences:- should introduce the main ideas of the paragraph.

SUBJECT:- is what we should talk about.

TOPIC:- the main points of the SUBJECT.

Write the topic sentence and two sentences supporting the topic.

SUBJECT	VERB	OPINION	TOPIC		
Body Paragraph 1	i) single	Being	has	many	**advantages.**

i) _____ .

ii) _____ .

| Body Paragraph 2 | ii) being single | However, | has | also many | **disadvantages.** |

i) _____ .

ii) _____ .

Chapter Four

Titles and Topics

Titles

- Titles must be written to stand out and be noticed.
- They are always connected with special words.
- These words are conjunction words; prepositions and articles. They must ALWAYS be written in lower – case, (small letters).

<u>**Conjunctions**</u>	<u>**Prepositions**</u>	<u>**Articles**</u>
and; or; but; so	on; in; with; behind above; below; over under; for, of	a, an, the

- The exception is when they are at the beginning of a sentence or in a *title.*
- *Titles* must always be complete, (you may lose or not get any marks for incomplete *titles*).
- *Titles* must ALWAYS be <u>underlined</u>, or written in **bold** so that they are

noticed. No periods to be used at the end of *titles* as they halt the flow.

An example:-

how to write an essay

<u>How to Write an Essay</u>

i) how to pass exams

. . . .

ii) our school is the best

. . . .

iii) my classmates and my school

. . . .

iv) how we get ready for school

. . . .

v) i knew i had passed

Titles & Topics

A *title* can be :-

i) The name of a book: ___**How to Play the Saxophone**___

2) The name of a film ___**Wuthering Heights**___

3) A piece of music: ___**Swan Lake**___

4) A word in front of ___**Sir**___ *Nick Faldo*
   someone's name: (page 2 rule 2)

The *title* however, need not be directly associated with the *topic*.
It must, however, have some kind of connection. For example:-

Title)	___**My Family**___
Topic 1)	***my parent(s)***
Topic 2)	***my sibling(s)***
Associated / Words	***father; mother; brother(s); sister(s);***

Put the *titles, topics* and *associated words* in their respective places.

1.   *food;_vegetables; fruit; carrots; cauliflower; onions; apple; pear; banana; strawberries; cherries; orange.*

      title   _____

      topic 1)   _____

      topic 2)   _____

      assoc;/words   _____

(page 27)

2.   *things with many parts; a house; a bicycle; kitchen; handlebars; bedroom; saddle; bathroom; wheel; lounge; brakes.*

      title   _____

      topic 1)   _____

      topic 2)   _____

      assoc;/words   _____

(page 28)

Topics

Topics are specific subjects that are to be discussed.
They give an idea to what is needed.

Understanding *Topics i*

A Name of a Specific Group
An example here is **footwear**.
There are a number of different kinds of footwear.

The subject could be written about the footwear they are likely to wear.
i. **Men's Sandals**, ii. **Youth's Trainers**, iii. **Ladies Boots**,
iv. **Men's Shoes**, v. **Children's Sandals**, vi. **Ladies Sandals**.
Write the specific name, under each picture.

Understanding *Topics ii*

Topics: that are names of groups

What is a *topic*? A *topic* tells what something is, about a title. It helps readers remember the title they have chosen. Here there are two kinds of *topics*. One is **the name of a group of things like** ....**FOOD** (1: Page 27)

another is **the name of a thing with many parts such as** ....**ROOMS in a HOUSE or BICYCLE PARTS** (2: page 28)

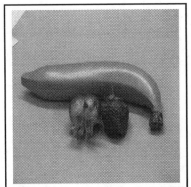

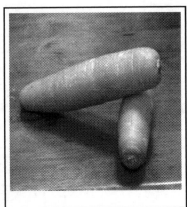

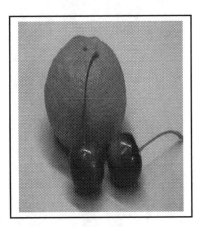

_____

_____

_____

_____

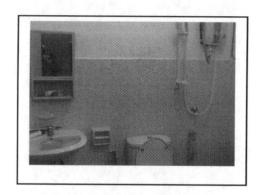

_____

_____

_____

_____

Finding *Titles* and Group *Topics*

Find the *Title* and *Group Topic* for each group of the associated words.

1. *Title:-* _____   *Topic:-* _____

    trees bushes fountain grass birds   _____

2. *Title:-* _____   *Topic:-* _____

    nose ears forehead chin cheek   _____

3. *Title:-* _____   *Topic:-* _____

    tooth-brush shower toilet bath shaver   _____

4. *Title:-* _____   *Topic:-* _____

    oven toaster fridge kettle kitchen-sink   _____

5. *Title:-* _____   *Topic:-* _____

    car bus train bicycle lorry   _____

6. *Title:-* _____   *Topic:-* _____

    grand-father niece uncle brother nephew   _____

7. *Title:-* _____   *Topic:-* _____

    morning evening midnight night dawn   _____

8. *Title:-* _____   *Topic:-* _____

    book magazine comic poem newspaper   _____

9. *Title:-* _____   *Topic:-* _____

    arm-chair settee coffee-table chandelier painting   _____

10. *Title:-* _____   *Topic:-* _____

    wardrobe bed pillow dressing-table bed-spread   _____

Choose any **number** from the above and **write** a *Topic Sentence.*

Subject Verb   *Opinion*   *Topic*

_____

Being Organised When Writing

Having a good organisational sense about writing is the key to having your work understood. Many languages divide their ideas differently and that is why it's important to arrange paragraphs, so that they flow, in an orderly fashion. We can start by organising places into groups.

Look at the list of places around the world in the list below. How are we going to put them in a logical order? First let's see if any of them are similar in any way.

Divide them into three groups.

A	B	C
Ghana		
Europe	_____	_____	_____
Spain		
Africa	_____	_____	_____
Shanghai		
Asia	_____	_____	_____
London		
Malaysia		
Durban		

1.   What do all the places in group **A** have in common?

_____.

2.   What do all the places in group **B** have in common?

_____.

3.   What do all the places in group **C** have in common?

_____.

Organising Lists

Organise each of the following groups by dividing them into three groups.

Tuesday   December

autumn   June

September   Saturday

spring   winter

Friday

Add extra items to the final lists.

A Name_____	B Name_____	C Name_____

jet   truck

bus   rocket

boat   sub-marine

car   ship

aeroplane

Add extra items to the final lists.

A Name_____	B Name_____	C Name_____

Organising Lists

Organise each list item into groups of two and then sub groups of four.

champagne	broccoli	chicken
beef	whiskey	lemon tea
carrots	lamb	beer
lemonade	potatoes	milk

A   A

Name_____   Name_____

A   B   C   D

Name_____   Name_____   Name_____   Name_____

Chapter Five

Topic Sentences

Topic Sentences

A paragraph is a group of sentences about the same *topic*. The main idea about the paragraph should be given in the first sentence. This sentence is called the *topic sentence*. It introduces the *subject* matter to be discussed and the information to be given to the other *supporting sentences*.

Constructing *Topic Sentences*

Topic sentences are constructed directly from the *title*. They are related to the *title* but may not necessarily be constructed using the same vocabulary. There are two ways of constructing *topic sentences*: Using the *title* or from *supporting sentences*. In an exam, the latter is sometimes used, to see if students really understand.

We use the *Wh*—words in order to give us some idea for the *topic sentence*.

In the 16 examples below, questions are asked for the title – *My Father.*

Fill in the blanks with questions for the title: My School Day.

Title	*My Father (example given)* / My School Day (exercise)
Wh-**at** (subject)	1) **What** job does he do? 2) **What** time does he go to work? 3) **What** time does he come home?
	*What*_____*?*
Wh-**y**	4) **Why** does he leave at a particular time? 5) **Why** does he work (reason) at a particular place?
	*Why*_____*?*
Wh-**en**	6) **When** did he start working there? 7) **When** does he have time to relax? 8) **When** does he find time to be with his family?
	*When*_____*?*
Wh-**ere** (place)	9) **Where** does he work? 10) **Where** does he go to relax?
	*Where*_____*?*
Wh-**o** (person/s)	11) Who does he work with? 12) Who does he drink coffee with?
	*Who*_____*?*
Wh-**ich** (selection)	13) Which shall we choose? 14) Which coffee does he like?
	*Which*_____*?*
How (method)	15) **How** does he get there and home? 16) How does he relax?
	*How*_____*?*

From the sixteen supporting ideas for the *topic sentences,* we will use some of the answers to construct a *topic sentence.* .These can also form our plan. Use one or two word answers.

What job does he do?

Doctor _____   _____

Why does he leave at a particular time?

Early practice _____   _____

When did he start working there?

Ten years ago _____   _____

Where does he work?

In town _____   _____

Who does he work with?

Two doctors _____   _____

Which nurses work with him?

Two doctors _____   _____

How does he get to work?

By bus _____   _____

My father is a hardworking doctor.

My father	is	a hardworking	doctor
SUBJECT	*VERB*	*OPINION*	*TOPIC*

Notice how the *topic sentence* is formed.
Write a sentence using your own answers.

_____

The latter, *supporting / concluding sentences,* are also formed from the above.

1. He leaves work very early.
2. He started working there ten years ago.
3. He works in town with two other doctors.
4. He travels every day by bus.
5. Therefore, he is a hardworking assiduous man.

Paragraph Puzzle

A. Title.
B. Topic Sentence.
C. Supporting Sentences.
D. Conclusion.

Sub ject	Ve rb	Opin ion	Opin ion	To pic	SUB JECT
Topic	Wh-	Wh-	Wh-	WH-	VERB
Opin ion	Wh-	Conc lusion	CONC LUSION	WH-	OPIN ION
Opin ion	Wh-	Conc lusion	Conc lusion	WH-	OPIN ION
Verb	Wh-	Wh-	Wh-	Wh-	TOP IC
Sub ject	Sub ject	Verb	Opin ion	Opin ion	Topic

A   My Dad

B.   My dad is a good dad.

C.   I have a lot of homework.
We study in my bedroom.
He listens to my problems,

D.   Therefore, I can always depend on him.

Creating *Topic* Sentences ONE Paragraph

Title	Subject	Verb	Opinion	Topic
My Family	My family	is		
My Parents	My Parents	are		
My Father	My father	is		
My Mother	My mother	is		
My Siblings	My siblings	are		
My Brother	My brother (s)	is/are		
My Sister	My sister (s)	is/are		

TWO
Paragraphs

Title	Subject	Verb	Opinion	Topic
My Family	My parent (s) My sibling (s)	is/are		
My Parents	My father My mother	is		
My Siblings	My brother (s) My sister (s)	is/are		
My Brother	My elder brother (s) My younger brother (s)	are		
My Sister	My elder sister (s) My younger sister (s)	are		
My Grandparents My Uncle/Aunts	My grandparent (s) My uncle/aunt(s)	is/are		

Topic Sentence Construction

From the following two paragraphs, construct the *Topic Sentence*. Read the paragraph carefully and answer the three Wh-questions. Remember how the *Topic Sentence* is formed, (use one or two words for your answers).

One of the penguins was ready to play. He waddled up the icy hill as fast as he could. Then he flopped onto his stomach and slid. Some of the penguins were eating lunch. They swallowed the fish as quickly as the zookeeper could empty the buckets of food. A few of the penguins were sleeping quietly. The children watched the penguins for a long time. When it was time to go, the children were sad. Many of the children liked the penguin exhibit the best.

1. *What*_____?
2. *Where*_____?
3. *Who*_____?

a. Write a *topic sentence*, using your answers

   SUBJECT   **VERB**   **OPINION**   **TOPIC**

_____

The students of Mrs. Jones's class were having a great time at the Zoo. Mrs. Jones suddenly remembered as they passed a restaurant sign, it was getting late and the children hadn't eaten. "Has anyone got the time"? She asked Jimmy to look at his watch. "It's 1.50", he said. "Oh no! We're supposed to meet Mr. Smith's class at 1.30. We're late!" They all started running towards the entrance.

1. *What*_____?
2. *When*_____?
3. *Who*_____?

a. Write a *topic sentence,* using your answers

   SUBJECT   **VERB**   **OPINION**   **TOPIC**

_____

Choosing a *Topic Sentence*

*Choose the best **topic sentence** for each of the following paragraphs and write it on the line provided.*

1).
   a. Rates and taxes should be expanded
   b. The council needs money to repair the coaches.
   c. The government has lots of cash.

Many of the coaches need repair work. Councilors tell everyone that there is not enough money to repair them. The council will have to get money from the government.

_____

2).
   a. Shopping is difficult.
   b. The supermarkets are very busy on particular days.
   c. It is wise to do a special day shopping much earlier.

It will be difficult, to shop, if you wait just before special days. Many Supermarkets run out of the most popular items, so it will be harder to find what you want. The supermarkets will also be crowded and waiting lines are much longer.

_____

3).
   a. Skiing is expensive.
   b. Skiing is loved by a lot of people.
   c. There are many problems to skiing.

Many people enjoy skiing, even though it's expensive and dangerous. A lot of people attend week-end skiing every winter. Many families go on skiing trips. Neither the high cost of skiing or equipment deters skiers away from the slopes.

_____

4)
   a. Travelling in the air has altered our lives.
   b. Advances in technology have made the world seem reduced in size.
   c. An important invention was the mobile phone.

A person can have breakfast in Sydney, board a plane and have dinner in Singapore. A businessman in Kuala Lumpur can place an order in Taiwan by picking up a telephone. A fan in China can watch his favorite soccer team in London, on television.

_____

Title and Topic Sentences

Read the following supporting sentences. Write a *title* and *topic* sentence for each story, (see pages **34 and 35**, for guidance).

1).

_____

_____

_____

They eat a lot of junk food and forget to eat fruit and vegetables.
As a result of this, there are many overweight school children.
Being over-weight is not good for their health

. . . .

2).

_____

_____

_____

It helps you to be alert in the morning. If you want to stay awake at night,
it helps if you drink coffee. However, if you drink too much coffee it won't
be good for your health. You might become addicted and can't live without it.

. . . .

3).

_____

_____

_____

My sister Jan is fourty-two. She is married to an architect and they
have two beautiful girls. She works very hard, as a nurse, at the local hospital
in Kuala Lumpur. A nurse must be a very kind and caring person.

. . . .

Chapter Six

Supporting Sentences

Identifying Topic and Supporting Sentences

Supporting sentences are what the name implies. They not only support the *topic sentences* but also the *concluding sentences*. Therefore they must be seen to be *linking, (and; but, conjunction words)*, the two together.

Supporting sentences must have a direct correlation with the *topic*. They must not deviate away from its essence otherwise the true meaning of the *paragraph* will not only be lost, but will also be ambiguous.

There are ways that this can be avoided. S*ignal* words (*First, Second, Next, Then, After That* and *Finally*), can be used in order to direct the reader from start to finish. They will not only help the writer but also the reader to understand what is going on. This method is used when writing about a *topic* with similar intentions and results. When writing about something you have done or are about to do, it's very helpful to picture the events as you write. Having been to or done something yourself, will *always* be helpful when writing.

After writing a title (remember to *capitalise* the words correctly, (page 2), picture the sequence in your mind (mind-mapping). Then complete the *linking sentences* (page 47), and write a *paragraph*.

Signal words may be adopted, but breaking up the first two *supporting sentences* further is more effective (page 36). This method also ensures that the writer has a better flow of information and direction. There is little danger of the reader being pulled away by *irrelevant sentences* (page 51). Use the *Wh—words*, (pages 34 - 35) when mind-mapping, to formulate the *supporting sentences*. When you pre-plan an essay this way, every *title/topic* will become as familiar as getting dressed.

Words that Signal a Text's Organisational Structure.

Students sometimes struggle to organize their notes to answer research questions. It might help them if they can understand certain words.

- **In the case of a research question**, students should begin on deciding on what type of question they need to answer.
- **In the case of a reading assignment**, the passage should be determined, early, on how it is to be organised.
- **In both cases**, students can look for some of the original *signal words* listed below, in helping them make up their minds.

Here is a list of *Signal Words*:-

Chronological Sequence

after, first, afterward, initially, next, following, immediately, finally, until, as soon as, before then, now, when, meanwhile, not long after, third, on, preceding.

Generalisation / Principle

additionally, most convincing, how to, moreover, conclusively, is caused by, typically, in order to, for this reason, effects of, if . . . then, steps involved , not only but also, furthermore.

Process / Cause and Effect

accordingly. as a result of, always , first, clearly, conclusively, furthermore, generally, however if, . . . then, in fact , truly, never, it could be argued that , typically, sometimes most convincing, third, secondly, rarely, not only but . . . also, typically, usually, often.

Comparison / Contrast

but, as well as, opposed to, yet, on, although, compared, still, on the other hand, in common, different from, however, similar to, even though.

Description

above, along, across, back / front of, appears to be, as in, behind, below, to the right/left, over , into, under, between, near, down, beside, on top of, outside. inside, in.

Linking Sentences: Words and Phrases

Addition
and
also
furthermore
in addition
too
again
the following
and then
what is more
moreover
as well as

Announcing/opinion
It would seem
one might consider/
suggest/propose/
image/ deduce/infer
to conclude

Summary
in brief
on the whole
throughout
in all

overall
to sum up
in summary

Illustration
for example
for instance
such as
as
as revealed by
thus
to show that
to take the case of

Cause & effect
consequently
thus
so
hence
as a result
because/as
therefore
accordingly
since
until
whenever
as long as

Emphasis
above all
in particular
notably
specifically
especially
significantly
more importantly
indeed
in fact

Sequence /Time
initially
first(ly)
then
so far
after (wards)
at last
finally
once
secondly
next
subsequently
meanwhile
at length
in the end
eventually

Comparison
equally
similarly
compared
an equivalent
in the same way
likewise
as with

Contrast/balance
but
however
nevertheless
alternatively
to turn to
yet
despite this
on the contrary
as for
the opposite
still
instead
on the other hand
whereas
otherwise

although
apart from

Persuasion (*Assuming the reader agrees*)
of course
naturally
obviously
clearly
evidently
surely
certainly

Restriction
only (if)
unless
except (for)
save for

Identifying Topic and Signal Words

i.   *Read the following sentences about Springfield Academy, a boarding school for high—school students. There is too much information for one paragraph. Some of the sentences are about the **quality** of the education and some are about the **rules** of the school. Label the former **Q** and the latter **R**. Identify the **topic sentences**, and write **signal words** that will make the paragraphs flow. (Refer to pages 47/ 48)*

1. _____ _____   The laboratories have the latest equipment.
2. _____ _____   Students are not allowed to leave without permission.
3. _____ _____   Students are required to wear uniforms.
4. _____ _____   The Academy is famous for its quality education.
5. _____ _____   Most of its graduates attend very good universities.
6. _____ _____   Many of the students of The Academy feel that the rules are too strict and old fashioned.
7. _____ _____   Students who do not maintain a B average, are put on probation.
8. _____ _____   A minimum of one hour of homework per class, is assigned.
9. _____ _____   Stereos and televisions cannot be played after 7.00pm.
10. _____ _____   No mobile phones are allowed during school hours.
11. _____ _____   The food is of the highest quality.
12. _____ _____   There is a lot of homework to get through.

ii.   *Divide the sentences into two groups*

1. Quality of Education	**2. Rules of the school**
_____	_____
_____	_____
_____	_____
_____	_____
_____	_____

Identifying Topic and Signal Words

ii   *Read the following sentences about a city. Two of the sentences are **topic sentences**; two are concluding sentences, the rest are **supporting sentences**. Divide them into two groups. Some of the sentences are about its advantages and some are about its disadvantages. Label the former A and the latter **D** . Then for each **topic**, write **signal words** that will make the paragraphs flow (Refer to page 47 / 48).*

1.	_____	_____	There are many places to eat.
2.	_____	_____	Many streets are traffic-jammed.
3.	_____	_____	A lot of big shopping arcades are available.
4.	_____	_____	Living in cities can be an *advantage*.
5.	_____	_____	Cities have congested roads with much traffic.
6.	_____	_____	There are many parking lots.
7.	_____	_____	Canals in the city's back alleys are usually dirty.
8.	_____	_____	But, living in these cities can also be a *disadvantage*.
9.	_____	_____	Arcades will usually provide lots of entertainment.
10.	_____	_____	Many cities have historical places to visit.
11.	_____	_____	There aren't many people who care about their rubbish disposal.
12.	_____	_____	The city's back alleys are usually rodent-infested.

ii   *Divide the sentences into two groups*

1. *Advantages* **Living in Big Cities**	**2.** *Disadvantages* **Living in Big Cities**
_____	_____
_____	_____
_____	_____
_____	_____
_____	_____

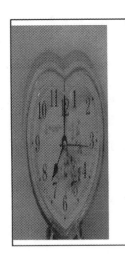

dressed, ran
clothes, hair,
downstairs,
breakfast

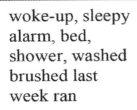

woke-up, sleepy
alarm, bed,
shower, washed
brushed last
week ran

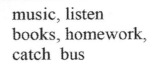

music, listen
books, homework,
catch bus

Plan

Paragraph 1	Paragraph 2	Paragraph 3
Who - Aishah	How - hurriedly	What - music tape
Where - bedroom	What - hair	When - before
When - morning	What - headscarf	Wednesday
last week	How - ran	What - bus
What - showered	What - breakfast	What - books
How - quickly		What - homework

Aishah *(who)* a second-year school girl, **woke-up** late, when she **went** to school *(where)*, **last week**. *(when)*. It was the *first* time she **was** late. Usually, she **walked** to the bathroom *(what, secondly)*, today, she **ran** and never **showered**, washed or **brushed** her teeth. Then also got dressed quickly. *(47 words)*

She quickly **dressed** *(how)* and put on the wrong socks and forgot her headscarf. Then ran **downstairs**, with un-brushed **hair** (what)? She had no time for **breakfast** that her mum had just made (when)? (35 words)

She forgot a **music** tape her teacher told her to **listen** to (when), before Wednesday. Also, her **homework** wasn't finished. (what)? On the **bus**, she remembered that she had the wrong **books** in her bag (what). *(39 words)*
(106 words)

Using Linking and Signal Words

You often find it difficult to keep your thoughts in order. Initially when writing paragraphs, it is sometimes best to use signal words that help you write, in a sequential manner (First, Second, Next, Then, After That, Finally).
Write a ***title,*** put the numbers sequentially against the appropriate pictures.
Then, write your own sentences in the correct sequence. Use *linking* words, and *signal* words, to construct a paragraph. Use the un-numbered pictures for additional ideas. For example, give reasons why she doesn't have to run for her bus. What does she have to do/not do to be on time for the bus?

Linking Sentences

Finish off the sentences from a – h.

    a) It's been very expensive, since_____.

    b) They never come on time, so_____.

    c) It's a very cheap restaurant because_____.

    d) It didn't look good, however_____.

    e) It's snowing, but_____.

    f) It's open late owing to_____.

    g) I'd love to help and_____.

    h) There's a train strike due _____.

The flow of a story can always be helped with the aid of *conjunction* words. Choose the correct *linking* word. Write another sentence using the same link word: underneath the sentence above.

    i) We will visit England .... Scotland next year.

    _____............ _____

    j) My back was aching............................ I went to see my doctor.

    _____............ _____

    k) I wanted to go skiing .... I couldn't get a flight in time.

    _____............ _____

    l) My brother was hungry .... he went and bought a sandwich.

    _____............ _____

    m) I want to pass my exams...................... I am always going to do my homework.

    _____............ _____

Chapter Seven

Irrelevant Sentences

SUPPORTING SENTENCES Recognising Irrelevant Sentences

Many students, when writing essays, waste a lot of time writing sentences
that are totally un-related to the *topic* of the sentence. They are **totally
irrelevant**. You must be focused upon the *topic* otherwise you get
sidetracked from your purpose.

i) **Write** the *topic* on the line; ii) **cross out** the **irrelevant one**;
iii) **write a suitable** *associated word* on the **line above**.

1. *Topic*___**Drinks**_____   **coffee**_____

       orange juice   tea   hot chocolate ~~sugar~~   lemonade

It does not belong, because **sugar is not a drink.**_____.

2. *Topic*_____   _____

       rabbit   budgerigar   tiger   goldfish   hamster

It does not belong, because_____.

3. *Topic*_____   _____

       study   kitchen   sitting room   garden   shed bedroom

It does not belong, because_____.

4. *Topic*_____   _____

       Tokyo   England   Somalia   Sudan   Libya

It does not belong, because_____.

5. *Topic*_____   _____

       fifteen   thirty-five   twenty-seven sixty   fourty-five

It does not belong, because_____.

SUPPORTINGSENTENCES Recognising Irrelevant Sentences

The following paragraphs contain one sentence that is **irrelevant.** Cross out the *irrelevant* one and explain why it should not be there.

1.   Cats make wonderful pets. They are loving and friendly. They are also clean. They don't eat much so they are inexpensive. ~~*Some have short tails*~~. They look beautiful. However some people are allergic to their hair. It *does not belong* because *having short tails isn't a reason why they should make good pets.*

2.   Learning the English language has many *advantages*. Most people in many countries speak it, therefore it's a good communication tool. It's widely used on the internet. My grandmother now speaks it. Many textbooks are written in English. It *does not* belong, because_____

_____

3.   Exercising has many positive effects on the body. First, it increases the efficiency of many body organs. Many people prefer to lose weight. Next, it will improve the physical endurance capabilities. Finally, this will increase the chances of wearing nice clothes. It *does not* belong, because_____

_____

4.   The Korean automobile industry uses robots in many phases of its industry. In fact, one large Korean auto factory is now using robots in all of its production. Some Japanese universities are developing medical robots to detect certain kinds of cancer. A few Japanese factories are using robots to paint their cars. Others are using them to test-drive. It *does not* belong, because_____

_____

5.   There are a lot of reasons why women are waiting until they are thirty-plus to have their first baby. Some have good jobs and want to continue their careers. Others don't want the responsibility. Many couples already have children. A few have seen how it ruined marriages. It *does not* belong, because_____

_____

Features of an _Irrelevant Topic Sentence_ (exercises)

Exercise 1

Read the following sentences and decide if they are _facts_ or _opinions_. The latter relate more to the topic sentence. They will enable you to generate supporting sentences. ~~Cross out~~ - ~~the wrong one.~~ Fact / Opinion.

1. An apartment is a set of rooms that are on the same level.   Fact / Opinion.

2. It's better to live on the highest floor.   Fact / Opinion.

3. A detached house is not one that is joined to another house.   Fact / Opinion.

4. Our apartment overlooked a small courtyard.   Fact / Opinion.

5. The neighbour's house had a rather nice bay window.   Fact / Opinion.

6. I don't think there was anyone living in the basement.   Fact / Opinion.

7. The housing estate is an area where there are a lot of houses.   Fact / Opinion.

8. The landlord is someone that you rent the house or flat from.   Fact / Opinion.

9. My landlord is a very fair person.   Fact / Opinion.

10. Our apartment is on the third floor.   Fact / Opinion.

Exercise 2

Read each _topic sentence_ and put a ✓ next to the ideas that are suitable and a ✗ next to the ideas that are not.

1.   My mother is always a hardworking woman.

_____ cleans the house every day.   _____ likes baking cakes

_____ goes shopping at week-ends.   _____ sleeps very late.

_____ helps us with our homework.   _____ cooks all the meals

2.   The library is a good place to read books.

_____ it helps us gain knowledge.   _____ must be good sighted

_____ saves money by renting   _____ improves vocabulary

_____ can read, anytime, anyplace   _____ can be hard or/soft back

3.   In the home useful animals are usually dogs.

_____ guard the house   _____ smell out drugs

_____ eat what they are given   _____ track missing people

_____ can do tricks   _____ loyal to their masters

Chapter Eight

Concluding Sentences

Writing a *Concluding Sentence*

Use this form to help organise your paragraphs. Write your **concluding sentence** in the final rectangle. Add any other words and details that you need to make it complete.

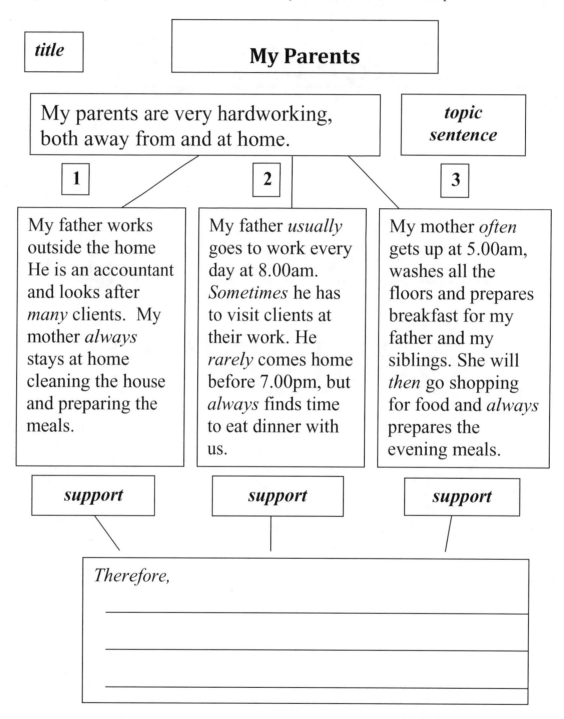

title	**My Parents**

My parents are very hardworking, both away from and at home.

topic sentence

1 **2** **3**

1	2	3
My father works outside the home He is an accountant and looks after *many* clients. My mother *always* stays at home cleaning the house and preparing the meals.	My father *usually* goes to work every day at 8.00am. *Sometimes* he has to visit clients at their work. He *rarely* comes home before 7.00pm, but *always* finds time to eat dinner with us.	My mother *often* gets up at 5.00am, washes all the floors and prepares breakfast for my father and my siblings. She will *then* go shopping for food and *always* prepares the evening meals.
support	*support*	*support*

Therefore,

_____

_____

_____

Notice how the supporting sentences in boxes two/three link up with the two sentences in box one. The conclusion box should also have sentences that relate to the main topic.

Writing a *Concluding Sentence*

Use this form to help organise your paragraphs. Write your **concluding sentence** in the final rectangle. Add any other words and details that you need to make it complete.

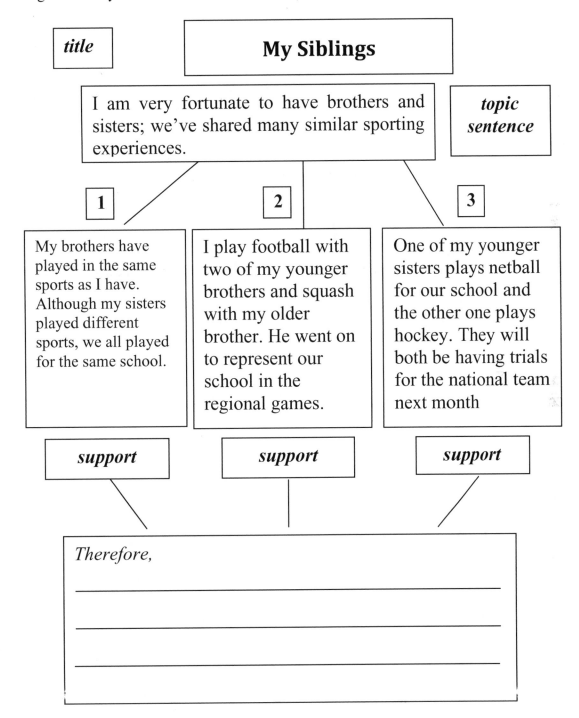

Concluding Sentences

*Complete the **concluding sentences** for each paragraph. Use the vocabulary in the body paragraphs. Pick out <u>**key words**</u> to help you*

Title　　　　<u>My City and Kuala Lumpur</u>

Topic
Sentence 1　　Living in a city can be an *advantage*.

Supporting
Sentences　　　　A lot of **big shopping arcades** are available in London and Kuala Lumpur. Also, cities provide many more places to **go and visit**. Regent Street and K.L.C.C. are where you can find all the **big stores** and you can **buy many bargains** in the sales. Arcades will also *usually* provide lots of entertainment. Both London and Kuala Lumpur are *often* full of **historical places to visit**, such as the Tower of London and the Batu Caves. Nelson's Column and other statues reflect their history.

_____

_____

Topic　　　　But living in London and Kuala Lumpur can also be a
Sentence 2　*disadvantage*.

Supporting
Sentences　　In both London and Kuala Lumpur there are **more public vehicles** also **people don't care** about their **rubbish.** Although London and Kuala Lumpur try to keep themselves clean, so much traffic *usually* **pollute** the air with their **fumes.** Buses and taxis as well as lorries, are the culprits. They also provide the **noise that is deafening**. Most large cities harbor the **selfish attitudes** of city-dwellers. They don't care about what happens to their immediate environment.

_____

_____

Concluding Sentences

Read the *supporting sentences* and then decide upon a suitable *title; topic sentence* and a *concluding sentence.*

A

_____

_____

_____.

First, I *often* get up late and eat breakfast. *Secondly*, I read a newspaper for a few hours. *Next*, by four-o-clock, I am *usually* hungry so I make myself a snack. *Then*, I watch TV and *sometimes* take a nap. *After that*, in the evening, I *often* go out to dinner with friends. I am *usually*, back in bed again by ten-o-clock. *Finally*, I like to relax on Sunday so that I am ready to start my week on Monday.

_____

_____

- -

B

_____

_____

_____.

First, she says *always* select the carrots that *sometimes* have their leaves still attached, because they'll be fresh. *Secondly*, buy some tomatoes that are almost ripe, *never* choose squashed or bright red ones. *Next*, I want some onions, Spanish, not spring, make sure they are *always* firm. *Then*, you can select potatoes, the King Edwards type. *Finally*, at the end of the counter, buy a tin of peas, that's where they are *usually* kept.

_____

_____

- -

C

_____

_____

_____.

First, it's a modern kitchen, nice and clean with a lot of cupboards. *Secondly*, there's a washing machine, fridge and a cooker. But there isn't a dishwasher. *Next*, there are some lovely posters on the walls, *however* there aren't any photographs. On the dining table there are some bananas and grapes.

_____

_____

Title			My Mother		

Thesis Statement	My mother *subject*	helps *verb*	me with my studies and gives me advice. *topic*		

Topic Sentence 1	My mother *subject*	is *verb*	*always* *opinion*	helping me	study. *topic*

Supporting Sentences	*When*	*When* I come home from school.
	What	She helps me with my homework and tells me *what* to do if I need help.
	Where	It's *usually* in our study, but she comes to the public library as well.
	How	*Finally*, she directs me to the correct books and talks to me in a calm manner.

Concluding Sentence 1 (Write your feelings)	*Therefore*, I can *always* rely on my mother whenI am studying.

Topic Sentence 2	_____ *subject*	_____ *verb*	_____ *opinion*	_____ *topic*

Supporting Sentences	*When*	_____ .
	What	_____ .
	Where	_____ .
	How	_____ .

Concluding Sentence 2 (Write your feelings)	_____ .

Now write an essay about **YOUR** sibling. Use the given *determiners,* or choose your own.

Title	_____			

Thesis
Statement
    _____   _____   _____
    subject   verb   topic

Topic
Sentence 1
    _____   _____   _____   _____
    subject   verb   opinion   topic

Supporting   *When*   _____
Sentences   _____.

            What   _____
                      _____.

            Where   _____
                      _____.

            How   _____
                      _____.

Concluding
Sentence 1   _____
                 _____.

Topic
Sentence 2
    _____   _____   _____   _____.
    subject   verb   opinion   topic

Supporting   *When*   _____
Sentences   _____.

            What   _____
                      _____.

            Where   _____
                      _____.

            How   _____
                      _____.

Concluding
Sentence 2   _____

Write about _____ and _____
Add *and / but* where necessary. Use frequency adverbs *always; sometimes* and *never*.
Use the space below to plan your writing. 120 words.

<table>
<tr><td rowspan="2">ThesisStatement</td><td><u>Subject</u></td><td><u>Verb</u></td><td><u>Topic</u></td></tr>
<tr><td>_____</td><td></td><td>_____</td></tr>
<tr><td><u>Quantifiers</u></td><td><u>Introduction</u></td><td><u>Body 1</u>
(topic)</td><td><u>Body 2</u>
(topic)</td></tr>
<tr><td rowspan="2">Many</td><td>What? _____</td><td>_____</td><td>_____</td></tr>
<tr><td>When? _____</td><td>_____</td><td>_____</td></tr>
<tr><td>Some</td><td>Where? _____</td><td>_____</td><td>_____</td></tr>
<tr><td>Quite a few</td><td>Who
with? _____</td><td>_____</td><td>_____</td></tr>
<tr><td>Not many</td><td>Why? _____</td><td>_____</td><td>_____</td></tr>
<tr><td></td><td>How?</td><td></td><td></td></tr>
</table>

Introduction
What? _____ *Who with?* _____ .

When? _____ . *Why?* _____ .

Where? _____ . *How?* _____ .

Body 1.
What? _____

When? _____ .

Where? _____

Who
with? _____
Why? _____

How? _____ .

Conclusion _____

Body 2
What? _____ .

When? _____ .

Where? _____ .

Who
with? _____ .
Why? _____ .

How? _____ .

Conclusion _____

Write about **Supermarkets** and **Street markets**

Add *and / but* where necessary. Use *frequency adverbs* always; sometimes and *never*.
Use the space below to plan your writing. Use the space below to plan your writing.

		Subject	Verb	Topic
Thesis Statement		***Many*** *people*	*use*	*street and supermarkets*
Quantifiers		**Introduction**	**Body 1**	**Body 2**
				(Street markets) (Supermarkets)
	What?	Street/Super markets	Food/clothes	*but* Food/clothes/electrical
Many/Most	*When?*	Week-end	Special days	*but* Anytime
Some	*Where?*	Villages	Anywhere	*but* *Usually* towns
Quite a few	*Who* with? families	Anyone *and*	Anyone	
Not many	*Why?*	Buy food	Cash/barter	*but* Cash/credit card
	How?	Private	Car / walk	*and* Car / bus
			no credit	can't barter

Introduction

What?   There are *many* street and supermarkets.
When?   *Some* people go to street markets during
          mid-week or week-ends.
Where? There are *always* markets everywhere.

Who?   *Quite a few* people frequent both.
Why?   *Many* go to street markets for bargains.
          Some go to supermarkets to buy on credit.
How?   Access can be by transport

Body 1
What?   Food and clothes can be bought in street markets, *but* clothes are not *often* bought because of the
          lack of changing rooms. Food is *usually* cheaper, because it's locally grown.
When?   Local markets have restricted times when they are available, *but not many* are open on a daily basis.
Where? Street markets can be accessed in both villages and towns, *but* again they may only be
          restricted to specific days.
Who?   *Some* people go to the market on their own, *and quite a lot* go to meet friends and neighbours.
Which? It is *often* a time to see old friends and for children to choose things.
Why?   At street markets, people can *sometimes* have prices reduced *but* there is no opportunity to purchase anything on
          credit.
How?   Access is *sometimes* by car, *and many* locals, walk as the market is not far from where
          they live.
Conclusion? Therefore, easy access, *most* street markets are restricted by their product choice.

Body 2
What?   Not only can food and clothes be bought at supermarkets, *but* a wide range of electrical goods also.
When?   Supermarkets are accessible every day of the week *and* stay open late.
Where? *Many* are available only in towns *and* not many can be located in villages.
Who?   *Usually,* families frequent supermarkets *and* the latter have play areas and *many* other shops that
With?   attract the larger family groups.
Why?   Supermarkets are attractive because of the opportunity for shoppers to buy things on credit, *but* even buying cash
          will not allow discounts to be entertained.
How?   Supermarkets will be accessed by car from very rural areas *and many* are accessed by
          public transport, in towns.
Conclusion? Therefore, accessibility is restricted by transport *but* the supermarkets' variety,
          make them popular.

Title [   ]

Getting Your Paragraph
                Organised

Introduction

[   ]

[   ] **Thesis**
                                                            Statement

Support   **Support**   **Support**

Conclusion

My City and Kuala Lumpur

Introduction

> Many cities have similar buildings. Some people of similar cities speak the same language. A lot of cities have rivers flowing through them. Quite a few cities have famous statues and buildings in them.

Thesis Statement

There are *advantages* and disadvantages to living in a city.

Plan

1. **Topic** **Sentence**	2.**Main** **Sentence**	3.**Sub-** **Sentence**	4. **Sub-** **Sentence**	5. **Concl /** **Sentence**
Living in London and *Kuala Lumpur can be an* **advantage.**	*Many* places to shop. *Able to visit many places.*	Shopping for many different things is made easier.	*There are far more places to see.*	*Therefore,* the city is more convenient and **advantageous**.

Topic Sentence

> Living in London and Kuala Lumpur can be an *advantage.*

Support

> A lot of big shopping arcades are available in London and Kuala Lumpur. *Also, cities provide* **many** *more places to go and visit.*

Support

> Regent Street and K.L.C.C. are where you can find all the big stores and buy many bargains in the sales. Arcades will also provide lots of entertainment.

Support

> *Both London and Kuala Lumpur are* **often** *full of historical places to visit. Such as The Tower of London and The Batu Caves. Nelson's Column and other statues reflect their history.*

Conclusion

> *Therefore,* I would rather live in a city to enjoy the shopping and history.

65

My City and Kuala Lumpur

Introduction

Many cities have similar buildings. *Some* people of similar cities speak the same language. *A lot of* cities have rivers flowing through them. *Quite a few* cities have famous statues and buildings in them.

Thesis Statement

There are advantages and ***disadvantages*** to living in a city.

Plan

1. *Topic Sentence* Living in London and *Kuala Lumpur can also be a* ***disadvantage***.	2. Main Sentence *Sometimes* it can be noisy, also it can be very dirty.	3. Sub-sentence Lots of traffic all day long.	4. Sub-sentence Canals and streets full of rubbish.	5. *Concl / sentence* *Therefore*, the city can be inconvenient and ***disadvantage ous.***

Topic Sentence

However, living in London and Kuala Lumpur can also be a ***disadvantage***.

Support	**Support**	**Support**
In both London and Kuala Lumpur there are more public vehicles *also people don't care about their rubbish.*	Although London and Kuala Lumpur try to keep themselves clean, so much traffic *usually* pollute the air with their fumes. Buses and taxis as well as lorries are the culprits. They also provide the noise that is deafening.	*Both London and Kuala Lumpur also have rivers and canals that are heavily polluted. Also the roads are not kept as clean and tidy as they should be. People are constantly throwing their rubbish out of car windows.*

Conclusion

Therefore, I would rather live in a city that is kept much cleaner than ours.

Title <u>My City and Kuala Lumpur</u>

Introduction

Many cities have similar buildings. *Some* people of similar cities speak the same language. *A lot* of cities have rivers flowing through them. But, some can be quite polluted. *Quite a few* cities have famous statues and buildings in them. Strewn rubbish piles can be seen in a lot of cities. The city can be very noisy during the day and night.

Thesis Statement

Living in a city has many advantages and disadvantages.

(71 words)

Topic Sentence

Living in a city can be an ***advantage.***

Supporting Sentences

A lot of big shopping arcades are available in Kuala Lumpur. Also, cities provide many more places to go and visit Regent Street and K.L.C.C. are where you can find all the big stores and you can buy many bargains in the sales. Arcades will also *usually* provide lots of entertainment. Both London and Kuala Lumpur are *often* full of historical places to visit. Such as the Tower of London and the Batu Caves. Nelson's Column and other statues reflect their history.

Conclusion Sentence

Therefore, I would rather live in a city to enjoy the shopping and history.

(105 words)

Topic Sentence 2

But living in London and Kuala Lumpur can also be a ***disadvantage.***

Supporting Sentences

In both London and Kuala Lumpur there are more public vehicles, also people don't care about their rubbish. Although London and Kuala Lumpur try to keep themselves clean, so much traffic *usually* pollute the air with their fumes. Buses and taxis as well as lorries, are the culprits. They also provide the noise that is deafening. Both London and Kuala Lumpur also have rivers and canals that are heavily polluted. Also the roads are not kept as clean and tidy as they should be. People are constantly throwing their rubbish out of car windows.

Conclusion Therefore, I would rather live in a city that is cleaner; to enjoy the beauty it has to offer.   *(126 words)*

My City and Kuala Lumpur

Many cities have similar buildings. *Some* people of similar cities speak the same language. *Alot* of cities have rivers flowing through them. But, some can be quite polluted. *Quite a few* cities have famous statues and buildings in them. Strewn rubbish piles can be seen in a lot of cities. The city can be very noisy during the day and night. *Living in a city has many advantages and disadvantages.*

Living in a city can be an advantage. A lot of big shopping arcades are available in London and Kuala Lumpur. Also, cities provide *many* more places to go and visit. Regent Street and K.L.C.C. are where you can find all the big stores and you can buy *many* bargains in the sales. shopping arcades will also *usually* provide lots of entertainment. Both London and Kuala Lumpur are *often* full of historical places to visit. Such as the Tower of London and the Batu Caves. Nelson's Column and other statues reflect their history. *Therefore, I would rather live in a city to enjoy the shopping and history.*

But living in London and Kuala Lumpur can also be a disadvantage . In both London and Kuala Lumpur there are more public vehicles also people don't care about their rubbish. Although London and Kuala Lumpur try to keep themselves clean, so much traffic *usually* pollute the air with their fumes. Buses and taxis as well as lorries, are the culprits. They also provide the noise that is deafening. Both London and Kuala Lumpur also have rivers and canals that are heavily polluted. Also the roads are not kept as clean and tidy as they should be. People are constantly throwing their rubbish out of car windows. *Therefore, I would rather live in a city that is cleaner; to enjoy the beauty it has to offer.*

Chapter Nine

Concluding Paragraphs

Title	<u>Aisha's Morning School Trips</u>
Introduction	Many schoolchildren have to get up early to go to school. Not many live near enough to be able to walk to school. School buses don't always wait for stragglers. Sometimes, pressure is then put on parents to get their children to school. Often missed breakfasts are related to poor achievements.
Thesis Statement	Getting ready for school early, has its advantages and its disadvantages. (74 words)
Topic Sentence 1	Aishah usually gets up on time to go to school.
Supporting Sentences	*First*, the alarm went off at seven-o'clock. She got up and went to have a shower in the bathroom. She always has a cold shower. Afterwards she brushed her teeth. Secondly, she got dressed and put on the freshly-ironed school clothes. Then, she ambled downstairs and had plenty of time to eat her favorite Nasi Lemak, her mother made her. After that, Aishah still had time to listen to her favourite music while she packed her bag with the correct books, she would need for the day. Finally, she went out the door as the school bus came around the street corner. (113 words)
Topic Sentence 2	Aishah sometimes gets up late to go to school.
Supporting Sentences	The alarm went off at seven-fifteen, she had set it wrong.. First, she couldn't wait for the shower. It was a bit faulty so she decided to wash in the sink. She cleaned her teeth with any tooth brush she found. Secondly, she got dressed and wore the school clothes, from the day before Then, she quickly ran down stairs, had no time to eat her favourite Nasi Lemak; listen to her favourite songs while she threw her school books into her bag. Finally, she tore out of the front door of the house. She almost missed the bus as it came around the corner. (115 words)
Concluding Paragraph	*Therefore,* not planning properly can result in many things going wrong. Aishah could have made sure her alarm was properly set. She could have pre-packed her books the night before, making certain that she had the correct ones. She could also have pre-hung the clothes she wanted to wear the next day. A little more thought in what she should have done would have made her life comfortable. (75 words)

Title	<u>A Chosen Celebrity</u>
Introduction	Celebrities are such because they are famous. *Many* would not be called such if *a few* people knew them. However even though they could be world-known, they might be unknown to some people. They are *usually* recognized when seen on TV. Actors, actresses and sportsmen will *often* be recognized, as well as singers and pop-stars, because of exposure.
Thesis Statement	I chose Roger Federer as my celebrity, for his tennis ability and his unassuming manner. (73 words)
Topic Sentence 1	Roger Federer has become a leading tennis champion.
Supporting Sentences	*First*, he became world junior champion in 1998. *Secondly* he has *always* consistently won titles. *Next*, in the 10 years to 2007, he couldn't stop winning titles. *Then*, he thrice won titles: the Australian Open, the U.S. Open and Wimbledon in the same year. He portrayed his ability to be able to excel in all the tennis crafts of the tennis game. *Finally*, in 2007 the Laureaus Sports awards named him, Sportsman of The Year for the third time. *Therefore*, by breaking so many records he also has a chance of surpassing Bjorn Borg's Wimbledon's record of five wins. (108 words)
Topic Sentence 2	Away from the tennis, Federer works to help those less fortunate than himself.
Supporting Sentences	*First*, he is *always* very sportsmanlike. He *never* argues about decisions that go against him and *usually* accepts them without fuss. *Secondly*, he established the Roger Federer Foundation to benefit **disadvantaged** children in countries like South Africa. *Next*, he encouraged other sports stars to raise money for those devastated by the tsunami. *Then*, in 2006 he became a Goodwill Ambassador for UNICEF. *Finally*, his first UNICEF visit was to Tamil Nadu in Southern India. *Therefore*, he epitomizes everything good about a person. (95 words)
Concluding Paragraph Re-phrase *Thesis Statement* Your opinions/ feelings, Therefore (1)	_____
Your opinions/ feelings I think (2)	_____
Your opinions/ feelings, It might be (3)	_____
Your opinions/ feelings It could be that, (4)	_____
Your opinions feelings, There should (5)	_____
Your opinions/ feelings, However (6)	_____

71

Title	<u>My Parents and I</u>
Introduction	A lot of *parents* are always busy. *Parents* try to be devoted to their children.
	Many *parents* are at home or are working away from home. try and share responsibilities in the home.
	Most *parents* have many responsibilities.
Thesis Statement	*My parents* are very important in my life. (47 words)
Topic Sentence 1	My father is *always* giving me advice.
Supporting Sentences	*First*, my father has *always* helped me through school and college. He is *usually* there when my homework gets too tough. He won't tell me the answers but I manage to work them out with his guidance. *Finally*, my father has reassured me regarding my future, as to what university
	I should attend. *Therefore*, having my father with me has meant I will *often* make the right decisions. (76 words)
Topic Sentence 2	I have a hardworking mother.
Supporting Sentences	*First,* my mother is a good cook. She *always* prepares delicious meals that I like. She *usually* buys fresh vegetables, to make certain of a tasty meal. *Next* she also maintains the household and it's *never* dirty. She washes my clothes and keeps my roomclean. *Finally*, she *always* finds time to talk to me. *Therefore*, having a mother like mine has helped me a lot, to understand that I must work hard to achieve anything (85 words)
Concluding Paragraph Re-phrase *Thesis Statement*	_____.
Your opinions/ *feelings, Therefore (1)*	_____.
Your opinions/ feelings I think (2)	_____.
Your opinions/ feelings, It might be (3)	_____.
Your opinions/ feelings, It could be that, (4)	_____.
Your opinions/ feelings, There should (5)	_____.
Your opinions/ feelings, However (6)	_____.

Title	<u>My Siblings and I.</u>
Introduction	Siblings have *always* helped to keep families together. They *sometimes*, have the same shared interests. Many *often* share in household responsibilities. Siblings of the same gender, quite *often* become close friends.
Thesis Statement	*Siblings* are very important in family lives.
Topic Sentence 1	I am always playing games with my brother..
Supporting Sentences	*First*, although we don't like the same teams, we *always* watch football matches together. My team beat his team last week, but we *never* quarreled about it. I can *always* ask my brother to play games with me. *Therefore,* we will *usually* be able to play games together.
Topic Sentence 2	I am also fortunate to have sisters.
Supporting Sentences	*First*, one has been like a second mother to me. She is *always* there to give me advice. My other sister is slightly *younger* than me. Although I don't share the same things as my brother, we still have similar interests. The three of us will *often* go shopping together at week-ends. *Therefore,* we all have a bond between us.

*Concluding
Paragraph*
Re-phrase
Thesis Statement   _____.
Your opinions/
feelings. Therefore (1)   _____.
Your opinions/
feelings. I think (2)   _____.
Your opinions/
feelings. It might be (3)   _____.
Your opinions/
feelings. It could be that, (4)   _____.
Your opinions/
feelings. There should (5)   _____.
Your opinions/
feelings. However (6)   _____.

73

Father

Introduction	Fathers, are the backbone to any family. The father *usually* makes the decisions. A father *rarely* cleans the house but *sometimes* might cook. Fathers generally provide the family income.
Thesis Statement	In this essay I will discuss the ***advantages*** and ***disadvantages*** of being a father.
Topic Sentence 1	My father has been supportive, *always* gave me advice and has helped me through my growing years.
Supporting Sentences	*First*, my father has *always* helped me through school and college .He *usually* took me to my primary school when I first started going to school. *Secondly* my father has watched me when I played football or rugby. *Then* my father is very understanding if I didn't come home on time and would explain the dangers involved. *Finally*, before I reached my teens he would explain some of the fine points of my adolescence.
Concluding Sentence	*Therefore* my father has contributed to an excellent start to my upbringing.
Topic Sentence 2	*In addition* I am very fortunate to have a father that understands my teenagehood.
Supporting Sentences	*First*, just before I went to college, my father helped me through my O-levels and A-levels. He gave me the confidence to achieve high grades. *Secondly*, these helped me choose the college I wanted to go to. *Next*, my transitions were made less complicated because of my father's patience. *Finally*, I *always* manage to find time to talk to him, about anything.
Concluding Sentences	*Therefore*, having a father throughout one's teenage life can be of great benefit, in understanding problems that one could encounter.
Topic Sentence 3	*However*, a friend of mine is very unfortunate to have a father that doesn't understand teenage hood.
Supporting Sentences	*First*, just before he went to college, his father didn't help him. He didn't give him the confidence to achieve high grades. *Secondly*, these didn't help him choose the college he wanted to go to. *Next*, his transitions were made more complicated because of his father's lack of patience. *Finally*, he didn't *always* manage to find time to talk to him, about anything. Not having a father throughout one's teenage life, can be a great discomfort, in understanding problems that you could encounter.
Concluding Sentences	*Therefore* the bond between us could *often*, be very strong. Or it could be weak, if we respect each other's roles in the family. This will *always* help to maintain stability. It will also give us good ideas. This could be emulated in one's own family. (367words)

(Note: These are five paragraphs. They're separated to emphasise distinctions).

Chapter Ten

Exercises

Topic Sentence Construction

A. Below is a *topic sentence*. Write good *supporting sentences* in the spaces provided. Make sure when you plan, you also . . . . .

- begin with a *title*.
- contain five or more sentences that support the *topic sentence*.
- end with *concluding sentence*.
- use correct *capitalisation; punctuation* and / *word order*.
- Use *frequency adverbs*.

The first day of school is always hectic because of the registration of new classes.

```
┌──────────────────────────────────────────────────────────┐
│                                                            │
│                                                            │
│                                                            │
│                                                            │
└──────────────────────────────────────────────────────────┘
```

_____

_____

_____

_____

_____

_____

_____

B. Read the paragraph below and then decide on a *suitable title; topic sentence* and *concluding sentence*.

_____

_____

   First, I *always* pack the things I need for the hike: the stove; cooking utensils and the tent. I may add a few tins of fruit and cartons of drinks. *Next,* I put a few clothes together, remembering to pack my swimming trunks because I *often* find a stream to swim in. *After that,* I collect my cheque and money. *Finally*, I get dressed in my hiking gear.

_____

_____

You are living in another country now. Write an email (100– 125 words) to friends, **telling them about your _Weekly Routine._**

Use the question words, below, to help you. Add _also / but_ where necessary.

Use frequency adverbs _always; sometimes_ and _never_, (where needed).

Use the space below to plan your writing.

Title _____

Intro _____
(Topic sentence
Support Sentences

What?	_____	_Why?_	_____
(subject)		(reason/s)	
When?	_____	_Where?_	_____
(time)		(location)	
Who with?	_____	_How?_	_____
(person/s)		(method)	

Do/Did _____
you like it,

_____

_____

_____

_____

_____

_____

_____

If you are living in city now. Write an email (100 – 125 words) to friends,

telling them about your –experiences

Use the following question words to help you. *What? When?; Where?; Who; How?*
Do / Did you like it?

Add *also / but* where necessary. Use **frequency adverbs** *always; sometimes* and
never. (where needed)

Use the space below to plan your writing.

	Subject	_Verb_	_Opinion_	_Topic_
Topic Sentence (1)	_____			
		also / but		
What?	_____		_____	
When?	_____		_____	
Why?	_____		_____	
Where?	_____		_____	
How?	_____		_____	
Which	_____		_____	
Who	_____		_____	

_____

_____

_____

_____

_____

_____

_____

_____

Daniel's Birthday Party

washing-up	sister	dancing	uncle
stereo	father	kitchen	mother
aunt	guitar	friends	drinking
taking pictures	coloured balloons	birthday cake	grand mother

Write a paragraph about Daniel's party. Use the words above to help you. Remember to also use, *capital letters* and the *correct punctuation*. You should include a *topic sentence; supporting sentences* and a *concluding sentence*. Where possible also include: *signal words* and *frequency adverbs*.

_____

_____

_____

_____

_____

_____

_____

_____

_____

Number the following **supporting sentences,** (number1-Topic Sentences have been filled in for each paragraph) Write a suitable **title; thesis statement and concluding sentence.**

_____

_____

_____ .

Paragraph 1

☐	*What / Where*	Then she goes to her first class. This is at 08.00 am.
☐	*What / Where*	First, she has a cup of coffee in the coffee shop.
1	*When / Where*	Maria, around 07.30 am, arrives at the university.
☐	*Where / How long*	She goes to the library, studies for 1 hour before lunch.
☐	*When / What*	She has another class, at 10.45 am. This is history.

_____

_____ .

Paragraph 2

☐	*Who / When*	They talk about homework & their plans for Saturday night.
☐	*When / What*	At 14.30, she has another class. This is geography.
☐	*Where / When*	Finally, she leaves the university after a long day, at 17.00.
☐	*Where / How long*	After the class they go back to the library, for 1 1/2 hours.
1	*When / Who*	Maria, at 13.15 with a friend, starts her afternoon session.

_____

_____ .

Write about _____ and _____
Add *and / but* where necessary. Use frequency adverbs *always; sometimes* and *never*. Use the space below to plan your writing. Write **three** paragraphs (about 150 – 175 words). Remember to include *topic; supporting* and *concluding sentences*. Also *signal words* where necessary. Use the plan and continue your essay on another piece of lined paper.

	Subject	_Verb_	_Topic_
Thesis Statement _____			
Quantifiers	**Introduction**	**Body 1** *(topic)*	**Body 2** *(topic)*
What?	_____	_____	_____
Many *When?*	_____	_____	_____
Some *Where?*	_____	_____	_____
Quite a few *Who with?*	_____	_____	_____
Not many *Why?*	_____	_____	_____
How?	_____	_____	_____

_____

_____

_____

_____

_____

_____

_____

_____

_____

_____

Satellite and Internet Television

Many people have strong feelings about the value of television, especially now that programs are available through the satellite over the Internet. There are people who suggest that increased access to these programs does more harm than good. However, there are also some who insist that it is a good thing.

*Complete the supporting sentences for the two body paragraphs and concluding paragraphs. Remember to include **frequency adverbs** where possible.*

Satellite and Internet TV does a lot of harm. _____

_____

_____

_____

_____

_____.

However, some say that they are both a good thing._____

_____

_____

_____

_____

_____.

Therefore,_____

_____

_____.

Writing essays can be easy if you follow these steps!
Start using your imagination and creativity to come up with some
ideas. Remember to use:—some facts; figures of speech; your opinions,
where necessary and a good use of the grammar you have been taught.
You will be marked accordingly but don't worry about not finishing
on time just yet. The important thing is to show you are aware of what
is needed to gain points.

Title:

Introduction:

General details _____.

Some _____.

Quite a lot _____

Not many _____

A few _____

Many _____.

Thesis Statement _____.

(main idea / subtopics)

Body 1:

Topic Sentence _____.

When _____.

Why _____.

What _____.

What _____.

Who _____.

Where _____.

Which _____.

Therefore _____.

Body 2:

Topic Sentence   _____.

When   _____.

Why   _____.

What   _____.

What   _____.

Who   _____.

Where   _____.

Which   _____.

Therefore,   _____.

Concluding Paragraph:

Therefore,   _____.

I think   _____.

It might be   _____.

It could be that   _____.

There should   _____.

However,   _____.

Content						Good Use of Grammar				
Titles	0	1	2	3	4					
Topics	0	1	2	3	4	Articles	0	1	2	3
Subject/Verb	0	1	2	3		Conjunctions	0	1	2	3
Supp'g Sent's	0	1	2	3	4	Capitals	0	1	2	3
Concl'g Sent's	0	1	2	3	4	Periods	0	1	2	3
Sub-Total_____						Spelling	0	1	2	3

Comprehension

						Sub-Total_____
Use of Tenses	0	1	2	3		**Comments**
Sentence Constr'n	0	1	2	3	4	_____
Use of Paragraphs	0	1	2	3	4	_____
Figures of Speech	0	1	2	3	4	_____
Sub-Total_____						_____

TOTAL   ⎡   / 100 ⎤

Summary

How to Write an Essay

Paragraphs	Sentences	Words
1) 75 (words)	6 –7	10—12
2) 100 (words)	8 –9	10—12
3) 100 (words)	8 –9	10—12
4) 75 (words)	6 –7	10 –12 (350 words)

I hope that this book has enlightened you to the practical ways of **writing essays.** I want to point out a few things when writing the **body** and **concluding paragraphs**.

1.   When deciding on the **topics,** for the **paragraphs,** it is important to make certain the **supporting sentences** are concurrent with the topic when **linking** them **(see page 45-46).**

2.   If the **linking words** are similar but **the topics** differ, you have to use **two body paragraphs** and a **concluding sentence** for both **topics,** **(see pages 56/57).** Here, there are many connotations to **the topics**.

3.   However, if there is a conflict in th*e* **topics,** then **two body paragraphs** must be used to emphasise the differences, **(see pages 58 to 68).** Here the emphasis is on how strong the argument is on the differences.

4)   The **concluding paragraph** could introduce other ideas and also leave readers to make up their own minds. The overriding decision maker could come in *a* **two or three sentence-concluding-paragraph**, that will summarise each paragraph. **(see pages 70—74).** Either way, I trust you will find enormous pleasure in putting your own ideas across, with the help of this book.

HAPPY WRITING!!

Phil Rashid

Bibliography

English for Malaysians
J.S Solomon' Chuah Ai Bee and Susila S Solomon
Pelanduk Publications

Ready to Write
A First Composition Text
Second Edition
Karen Blanchard & Christine Root

English Language Workbook
Early Learner Publications Sdn. Bhd

Punctuation and Spelling
A Writer's Bureau Handbook 2000

How to Write an Essay. Original full-length version

Edited by: Dr Yahaya Abdullah, Siti Hajar Husna
Mariatolkabtiah binti Ithnin

NOTES

NOTES